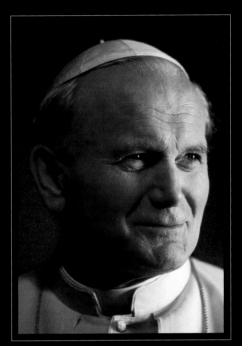

"When, on 22nd October 1978, in St. Peter's Square, I said the words, 'Do not be afraid!',
I did not fully realize how far they would carry me and the whole Church."

Joannes Paulus II

JOHN PAUL II
The Pope Who changed the World

Photographs
Gianni Giansanti

Texts
Valentina Alazraki

Editorial coordination
Ada Masella

vmb
PUBLISHERS

CONTENTS

NUORO, October 1985. A moment's pause – or reflection – during an encounter with the citizens of this Sardinian town.

SARAGOSSA, 1985. Measured, solemn: John Paul II seems to want to embrace the world, during the awe-inspiring period of his great apostolic journeys.

THE 26 YEARS OF THE PONTIFICATE

For over a decade, the Wojtyla hurricane shook the world. Grasping his pastoral letter as a crusader grasps his sword, John Paul II took his message to the five continents; he had crosses raised in places where a cross could never have been raised; he turned the center of Christianity into a moving point. His extraordinary human and religious adventure began with a few simple words, which over the years took on a deep prophetic connotation: "Open your doors to Christ!"

I was in the square that evening in 1978 when, having just been elected Pope, Wojtyla said, "If I make a mistake, you will correct me…"

I was twenty at the time, and like all the faithful who were watching the central loggia of St. Peter's Basilica, I was immediately won over by that humanity, combined with such a strong will to act, to be committed.

And I understood that the new Pope whom I was photographing would play a big role in my life, and in the history of the world.

From that moment on, not a year has gone by in which I have not followed the Pope, whether at the Vatican or on his numerous trips: I saw him fighting to change history, breaking down the wall of Communism; I documented his tireless activity to take the Church to those places where poverty, war and injustice reign; I saw his commitment to encouraging encounters with other religions; I heard him ask forgiveness for the wrongdoings that the Catholic Church committed in the past; and I saw him suffer and cry, sometimes for the woes of the world, sometimes for the times, too often, when his personal physical sickness threatened to force him to stop — although it did not succeed in doing so until that sad evening of Saturday, April 2nd, 2005.

Apart from anything else, this book, which is a photographic account of the pontificate of John Paul II, aims to be above all my homage to the man who, more than any other, has inspired my photographs; it is also a thank you for the opportunities he gave me, thanks to his courage and strength, to observe the world changing at first hand.

Gianni Giansanti

VATICAN CITY, 16 October 1978. "If I make a mistake … if I make a mistake you will correct me," the Pope says, from the central balcony, on the day of his election.

The Swiss Guards salute the new Pope as he makes his entrance into the Vatican through the Arch of the Bells. THE VATICAN, October

Two wings of the crowd block the car in a street in Kinshasa, and for the Pope it is the perfect chance to hug a child. ZAIRE, October

1980

Papa Wojtyla, kneeling before the Peace Memorial in Hiroshima, prays for all the victims of nuclear war. JAPAN, February **1981**

At Avila, the Pontiff admits that "At times like that of the Inquisition, tensions, mistakes and excesses took place." SPAIN, May

1982

1983 LOURDES, August Children, who are the most affectionate and unrestrained of the Pope's flock, wave handkerchiefs, thrilled by his unexpected visit.

A native woman in Mount Hagen greets the Pope on behalf of the "mountain people." PAPUA NEW GUINEA, May

1984

1985

CASABLANCA, October. The King of Morocco, Hassan II, invited John Paul II for a meeting at his contemporarily...

1987

1988 BOLIVIA, May A final goodbye from the aeroplane steps before returning to La Paz.

1989 THE VATICAN, March St. Peter's Square, enclosed by Bernini's great colonnade, is where great religious celebrations take place.

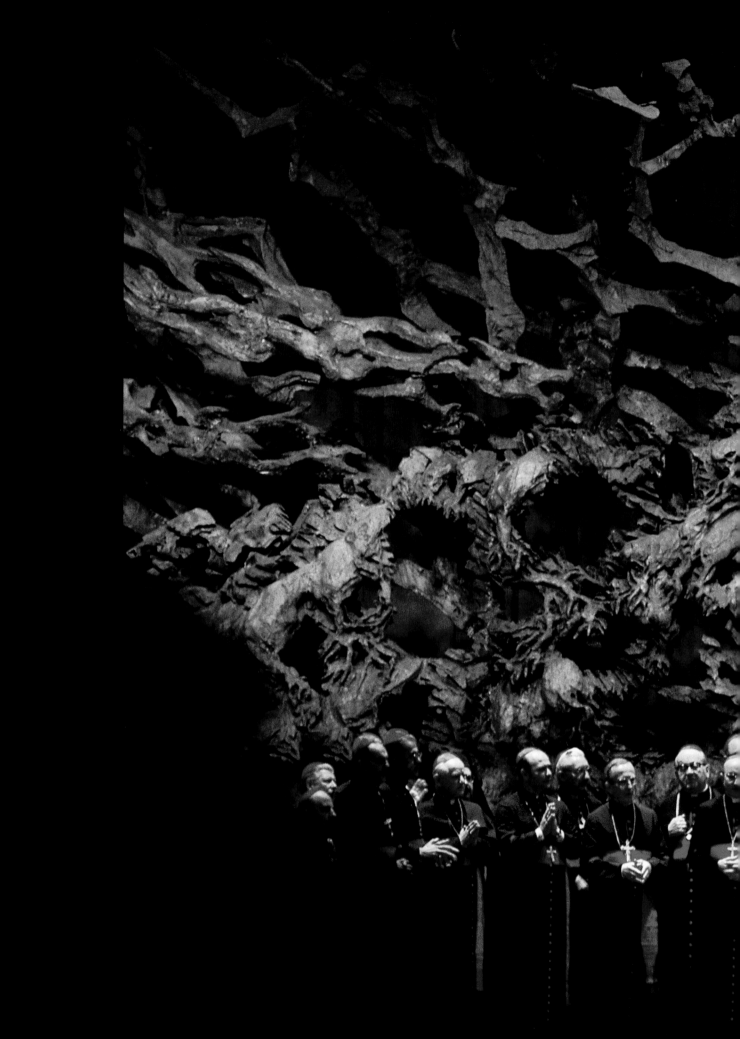

In the summer months, the traditional weekly meeting with the believers took place in St. Peter's Square. THE VATICAN, June **1991**

Pilgrims from all over the world crowd into St. Peter's Square to watch the beatification of Escriva de Balaguer. THE VATICAN, October

1992

1993 LITHUANIA, September The visit to the Hill of Crosses, a national shrine, on occasion desecrated, but always faithfully reconstructed.

1994 THE VATICAN, November The Pope places the cardinal's biretta on the head of the Bishop of Sarajevo, Monsignor Vinko Puljic.

1995 NEW YORK, October The UN General Assembly, packed with representatives, listens to the Pope's speech on the "Bill of Rights of Nations."

1996
ITALY, April One of the Pope's most stirring ceremonies in Rome, during Easter, was the Via Crucis procession in the Colosseum.

1997 BOSNIA HERZEGOVINA, April The "popemobile" passes in front of a wection of land that has become a cemetery for war victims.

1998 CUBA, January At the José Martí airport in Havana, the Pope meets the Communist leader Fidel Castro.

After years of restoration, the Pope reopens the Sistine Chapel; in the foreground is a detail of Charon and the Damned. THE VATICAN, December

1999

With Yassir Arafat, at the Dheisheh refugee camp, the Pope recalls the torment that the Palestinians have suffered. PALESTINE, March **2000**

The moving visit with the nation's Orthodox leaders to the Tzitzernakaberd Memorial in Yerevan, ARMENIA, September

2001

2002 MEXICO, July The dancing of the Indios accompanies the canonization of Juan Diego Cuauhtlatoatzin in the Basilica of Nuestra Señora de Guadalupe.

The Pope delivers the *"Urbi et Orbi"* blessing on Christmas Day. THE VATICAN, December 2003

2004 SWITZERLAND, June The "popemobile" crosses Allmend Park in Berne, after the Mass for National Catholic Youth Day.

ITALY, February. John Paul II leaves the Gemelli Hospital in Rome, where he was admitted twice in one month.

THE POPE'S DAILY LIFE

Each day, pictures and news of the Pope reached people all over the world: during his trips; meeting heads of state and representatives of other religions; in St. Peter's Square conducting religious ceremonies. However, it was not easy to find out what the Pope

The Pope's day always began with a Mass at 7.00 a.m. in his private chapel, a sober, secluded place. It was celebrated in Italian, in Latin, or, as a sign of courtesy, in the language of the most numerous group present. The lucky few were contacted directly by Monsignor Stanislaw Dziwisz, John Paul II's private secretary; he would phone them a few days beforehand and ask them to arrive at 6.30 a.m. sharp at the bronze door, at the end of the right-hand colonnade in St. Peter's Square. The Swiss Guards would then check their names on a short list that did not usually exceed twenty people. In a spectral silence, due partly to the early hour, they were led upstairs to the courtyard of St. Damasus, where there is a lift to the third floor.

There, they were taken into the library, where Don Stanislaw did the honors. When they finally entered the private chapel, the Pope was there already, sitting or kneeling in meditation. The Mass was also attended by the two secretaries and the Servants of the Sacred Heart, the Polish nuns who assisted the Pontiff in his daily life; these included Sister Tobiana, who in recent years had also begun to accompany the Pope on trips abroad in order to care for him. After the celebration, the guests were taken into the nearby library, to wait for the Pope to arrive and exchange a few words with each of them.

After Mass came breakfast. In the past, a Pope's solitude was especially evident during mealtimes. John Paul II also valued solitude; the point of this solitude was to search continuously for contact with God, and he broke with tradition, turning his table into a meeting place to discuss work issues or listen to bishops who had been summoned to inform him about specific situations in their dioceses.

The table at which the Pope – on his own on the right side – and his guests sat at was simple: rectangular, a white tablecloth, white dishes with a gold border and the papal coat of arms.

The menu was simple. The Polish nuns saw to it that Wojtyla's favorite dishes were always on the menu, and there was always a *"rosetta,"* the best-loved type of Italian bread.

Dinner, at around 8 p.m., was a quieter and more solitary affair than lunch. It was also a more frugal meal. His collaborators report that, before sitting down to eat, John Paul II listened to the evening news headlines. They also say that every now and then, he liked to watch a football match. During the 1986 football World Cup in Mexico, I had the opportunity to ask him if he was going to watch any matches, at least those of Italy and Poland. With his typical good humor, he answered that he would do if his collaborators allowed him to, but he didn't go so far as to reveal which team he would be supporting.

After breakfast, the Pope spent a couple of hours working in his study: he read, wrote and prepared documents, and every now and then would visit the chapel opposite his study, in order to find inspiration in prayer.

At 11a.m the audiences began, becoming less numerous and shorter over the years. The Pope would receive ambassadors, bishops visiting *"ad limina apostolorum"* (every five years bishops have to come to Rome, to the tomb of Peter and Paul, to present the situation of their dioceses), nuncios, political figures; while in the afternoon, after 5 p.m., he received the various ministers in turn and, of course, his close collaborators in the Secretariat of State.

History took place in the Pope's library and private study; history was made in these places, which have become one of the most important settings of the world, where John Paul II held very high profile and sometimes improbable meetings behind closed doors; such as when he received the electrician from Gdansk, Lech Walesa, as President of Poland, or Gorbachev for the first time, on 1 December 1989, or Fidel Castro in November 1996.

The audiences were not held on Tuesdays and in the first few years, the Pope took advantage of this to make some "secret trips," which only became public knowledge the day after; one of his more famous "escapades" was when he went with Alessandro Pertini to Mt. Adamello. The former president of

"But Your Holiness, you turn like a swallow!"

Italy, having watched the Pope ski, exclaimed, "But Your Holiness, you turn like a swallow!" Nor were the audiences held on Sundays, because the Pope generally dedicated the day to visiting a parish in Rome or to a celebration at St. Peter's to mark a beatification or canonization, or other event. However, a constant event on Sundays was the recitation of the Angelus or Regina Coeli from the window of his private study: this occasion was sometimes marked by extremely dramatic moments, such as on one July morning in 1992 when John Paul II, going against tradition and breaking one of the Vatican's most deep-rooted taboos, calmly revealed to the world that he was going into hospital for some health checks. These checks later revealed a tumor; memorably, on Christmas morning, having not celebrated mass due to a cold, John Paul II wanted to appear at all costs to deliver the *Urbi et Orbi* blessing; but an indisposition prevented him from doing so and he himself said, "I must stop."

Meanwhile, the Wednesday audience was "general," open to all, and took place in St. Peter's Square, weather permitting (otherwise it was transferred to the Paul VI Hall): it was during one of these audiences in the square, on 13 May 1981, that John Paul II fell victim to an assassination attempt carried out by a Turkish national, Ali Agca. The event kept the world in suspense. The

attack did not have fatal consequences: Agca missed his aim – for the first time ever, he later stated, and in his own words it was this "miracle" that led him to convert to Christianity. But physical pain had already started to trouble the Pope.

In the months prior to the discovery of the tumor, cameramen and photographers had already captured expressions of suffering on the face of John Paul II; the same thing happened after he broke his femur in 1994, and when he underwent an operation for appendicitis, in 1996.

Pain and sickness had also partly modified his life in the Apostolic Palace, as well as his holidays; no more of the walks in the Vatican gardens, with which he used to begin his afternoons. No more of his beloved walks in the mountains, in the solitude of the woods; a minimum amount of movement, now almost always taking place on the mobile platform which caused such amazement when we first saw it and told us that there were to be many changes in the organization of the Pope's movements. Even his official audiences, which were always held on the second floor, were moved to the private apartment.

Yet that pain which was by now constant for the Pope, who was physically undermined but increasingly courageous, strengthened his soul. He was determined to guide the Church to the very end, for as long as God wished, and he did not spare himself or give up dreaming of new trips. The number of days he spent outside the Vatican show clearly that, compared to life in the Apostolic Palace, the Pope preferred being among people in foreign, even far-flung countries, to remind them that the Church exists, and that he was its leader. The Pope wanted to spend time among the people, to absorb the joy and happiness, the liveliness and human warmth that he had always encountered all round the world, and that had made him realize that he could not remain a "prisoner" in the Vatican. He himself once explained that "Christ did not tell us to sit in the Vatican, he said: 'Go into all the world and unto the ends of the earth.'"

6.15 a.m.

MORNING PRAYERS

As he did every morning, the Pope secludes himself
in meditation in the private chapel, while a nun
prepares the altar for the morning Mass.

7.30 a.m.

THE GATHERING

Mass began at 7.00 a.m. in the small chapel. Every
morning, a few guests are invited to follow the service.

8.10 a.m.

THE MEETING

After celebrating Mass, the Pontiff used to meet his guests
in the nearby library, and exchange a few words with them,
sometimes humorously.

BREAKFAST

John Paul II eats a frugal breakfast while Cardinal Stephen Kim shows him details of the program for the forthcoming Papal Visit that the Pope was going to make to South Korea.

11.00 a.
RETURN HOM

After a short meeting, the Holy Fat

returns to his private apartments throu

the Raphael Loggia,the windows of wh

look directly onto the courty

of St. Damas

25 a.m.

PEECHES

ok out onto the Eternal City through

windows of his bedroom, during a break

n work, before making a live televised

ech from the library.

12.10 p.m.

CONFESSION

The Pontiff's confession took place each year and was part
of Easter celebrations: it was one of the occasions that
the faithful looked forward to most, and crowds of them flocked
to the Basilica for the occasion.

12.00 pm

THE ANGELUS

Pope John Paul's regular Sunday
appointment with the faithful gathered
in St. Peter's Square: the Angelus was
given from the window of this study.

4.20 p.m.
THE WALK

After leaving St. John's Tower, where the Pope
lived at the beginning of his papacy, a short
walk through the Vatican gardens provided a
chance to read some official papers.

6.45 p.m

PRAYER

Upon his return to the Apostol

Palace, Pope John Paul usually spent

few moments deep in prayer in th

Hall of Clothing

THE PAPAL JOURNEYS

The Pope, a tireless traveler, was convinced that Rome, the heart
of a Church of pilgrims, is no longer in Rome, but in the streets of
the world; he took the Christian message across the continents,
meeting his flock and making interreligious dialogue one of the

"A Polish song says, "You need to cross the world." It was a dream. How can I get to that world, I wondered, if it is all closed, if there are Communists in power, if there is the Iron Curtain? Whereas the Lord, with his mother, brought us here to Rome, and then from Rome to the world. And so, with the journeys across the world, I understood that to be a modern, updated Pope, I had no choice but to travel, in the present-day way of traveling, which is by plane." With his breviary as his inseparable travelling companion, John Paul II had in fact turned the aeroplane into a new wing of the Apostolic Palace. He prayed in it, read, rested, lunched, dined and even "confronted" journalists in it. He returned to the plane at the end of each journey, sometimes reluctantly because, as he once said, "Travel yes, but always to return!"

The days when John Paul II was described as the "marathon runner of God, the athlete of the Lord, the globetrotter of faith" seem a long time ago now. Yet, for over a decade, the Wojtyla hurricane shook the world. Grasping his pastoral letter as a crusader grasps his sword, John Paul II, in love with Christ, took his message to the five continents; he had crosses raised in places where a cross could never have been raised; he turned the center of Christianity into a moving point. His extraordinary human and religious adventure began with a few simple words, which over the years took on a deep prophetic connotation: "Open your doors to Christ!"

Just three months after saying these words from the central loggia of St. Peter's Basilica within minutes of his election, John Paul II began his itinerant ministry in Mexico. It was there, among millions of people thronging the streets, that John Paul II understood what kind of pope he wanted to be; he discovered that his place was not in the Apostolic Palace, but anywhere in the planet where he could give a voice to those who generally do not have one. This is what gave rise to his apostolic anxiety, the strong feeling of missionary "urgency" in a world that is too distant from God.

Moved by what he himself defined as "a slightly geographical" spirituality, John Paul II saw his ministry as an apostolic marathon, as a missionary campaign in which not only his words echoed, but also his shouting in favor of the oppressed, the forgotten and all those

victims of human rights violations, especially the right to religious freedom.

His apostolic and missionary dynamism earned him some criticism: he was accused of being superstar Wojtyla, of seeking out triumphalism rather than true participation, of carrying out a myriad of meetings that were too short, of leaving little room for reflection. During his journeys, John Paul II surprised the world with his harsh tones. Never had such an angry, indignant Pope been seen as at Managua, when he shouted back in reply to the Sandinista demonstrators. His voice thundered against the powerful, the rich, the corrupt, against false idols, against regimes that forbid the presence of God in society, against mafiosi of every type. He let his cry against war be heard, he personally visited countries at war and helped create the dream of democracy in countries ruled by dictatorships.

The Pope's commitment to peace through his trips was undoubtedly one of the dominant aspects of his mission. It took courage to go to Argentina or the United Kingdom during the Falklands (or Malvinas) War. Yet Wojtyla decided to go there despite the risks. On his first trip to Poland, which turned out to be "revolutionary" and shook the foundations of the Soviet empire, John Paul II declared, in Warsaw's Victory Square, that "Christ cannot be excluded from the history of mankind in any part of the world"

of the Lord, the globetrotter of faith...

because "the exclusion of Christ from the history of mankind is an act against mankind." During a visit to Liechtenstein, he said, "Where was God at Auschwitz, at Hiroshima, at Nagasaki? Where is God when children are starving to death, when men and women are tortured, when young people full of hopes must die?"

But we cannot mention the journeys of John Paul II without remembering his encounters with young people. It was with them that the Pope shone at his brightest, because he had always felt young at heart and had always loved spending time with young people, traveling with them, singing with them, studying with them.

During his journeys, we saw at first hand some of the most important and moving moments of Wojtyla's papacy. In Cuba we all had the impression that we were playing a role in history, as witnesses to an event that just a few years earlier would have seemed impossible. On the plane that took us to Havana, in response to our questions regarding human rights, the Pope was extremely clear. "Human rights are the cornerstone of every civilization"; he also said that he wanted to hear "the truth" from Fidel Castro, as a man, as a president, as a commander. "I want him to tell me the truth about his country!"

The meeting between the Communist leader and the leader of the Church, between "the devil and the holy water," as some Vatican scholars said, was a meeting between two warriors, two revolutionaries, even if they came from opposing sides: a meeting between the last two great charismatic leaders of the 20th century.

John Paul II had ardently desired to travel to the Holy Land ever since the first Christmas he celebrated in the Vatican. This journey was above all, proof of the courage of a man who, before many diplomacies did so, recognized the Palestinians' right to have a homeland, and who decided to change the Church's position on Israel and Judaism. In the birthplace of Jesus, the Pope's words rang out as he said "enough" to the desperation and depression of a people without a homeland.

"Your torment," said John Paul II to the Palestinians, "can be seen by the whole world, and has gone on long enough." He then became even more explicit. Upon arrival in Bethlehem, he kissed the ground of Palestine as he always did when he arrived in a sovereign country.

However, the most intense and stirring moments took place in Jerusalem, in the Yad Vashem, the Holocaust memorial, and at the Wailing Wall.

At the memorial, the black stone walls will preserve forever the indescribable emotion, the silence, the tears of the Pope, who begged for "no more anti-Semitism." John Paul II, the first Pope ever to have set foot in a synagogue, assured the Jewish people that the Catholic Church "is deeply saddened by the hatred, acts of persecution and displays of anti-Semitism directed toward the Jews by Christians at any time and in any place." The image of the Pope inserting a note into the Wailing Wall will become part of the history of his pontificate. This was one of his great intuitions: in one of the most symbolic places in the world, John Paul II left his *mea culpa* for the persecution of the Jews. "God of our fathers, you chose Abraham and his descendants to bring your name to the nations: We are deeply saddened by the behavior of those who in the course of history have caused these children of yours to suffer, and asking your forgiveness, we wish to commit ourselves to genuine brotherhood with the people of the Covenant."

Never was there a prediction more wrong than that which said that, after the year 2000, Jean Paul II would stop traveling. On the contrary, the Pope stepped up his ecumenical commitment and set about visiting many former Soviet republics or former Soviet realms in order to create a dialogue with the Orthodox Church.

In his first journey of the new millennium, John Paul II, in the footsteps of St. Paul, went to Greece; he did not manage to avoid provoking hostility among the most extreme Orthodox groups. He received a cold welcome from the Archbishop of Athens, Christodoulos, who confronted him on his arrival with accusations regarding the schism of 1054; nevertheless, he managed to turn the situation around with a solemn mea culpa that earned him a round of applause from the Archbishop and his entourage.

The Areopagus, where St. Paul spoke in the year 50 A.D., then became the setting for signing a common declaration in which the

Catholic Church and the Orthodox Church condemned "all recourse to violence, proselytism and fanaticism in the name of religion."

Still following the footsteps of St. Paul, the Pope moved from Greece to Syria, where a Pontiff visited a mosque for the first time ever. Wearing white slippers, accompanied by the Great Mufti of Syria, Almod Kuftan, he entered the Omayyad mosque, trembling and his head bowed; after having prayed before the Memorial to John the Baptist, he crossed the mosque with 86 year-old Mufti by his side, who was also unsteady on his legs. Once they had gone out of the temple and sat in the courtyard, beneath the "Minaret of Jesus," John Paul II asked to forget the reciprocal offences. "For each time that Muslims and Christians have offended each other, we must ask the forgiveness of the omnipotent and offer forgiveness to each other."

Upon his arrival in Damascus the Pope had requested respect for the United Nations resolutions on the Middle East, with a speech that was interpreted as a condemnation of Israel's policies; in Kuneitra, a ghost town that was destroyed by Israel, he invoked peace and asked to "knock down the walls of hostility and division."

Great openness toward Eastern Europe and beyond also marked the Pope's journeys in the second millennium. His trip to

Azerbaijan and Bulgaria was a journey of suffering. For the first time, John Paul II had to use a lift to get on and off the aeroplane, and a mobile platform for moving around. This was also the first trip on which he was unable to read out his speeches himself. At the end of the visit, the Vatican spokesman Joaquin Navarro-Valls stated that John Paul II had decided to incorporate all of his suffering into his itinerant ministry and to go on until the end. In fact, when in Baku, he said, "I will shout in favor of peace for as long as I have a voice."

He had much more strategic reasons for visiting Bulgaria, the last stop on his approach to Moscow after having made visits to Georgia, Ukraine, Kazakhstan, Armenia and Greece. In Bulgaria, during his meetings with the Orthodox Patriarch Maxim, the Pope expressed his hope that one day, a perfect unity of thought and intention would be reached through a deeper mutual understanding. The Bulgarian Orthodox were initially reticent, and were opposed to any instance of common prayer; but despite this, in the Monastery of Rila, the most sacred place of Bulgarian Orthodoxy, John Paul II stretched out his arms not only to them, but also to the monks of Mt. Athos, particularly those from Russia. "What would Bulgaria be without the Monastery of Rila, what would Greece be without holy Mt. Athos? Or Russia, without that myriad of homes of the Holy Spirit which made it possible to overcome the hell of Soviet persecution?" the Pope asked. He said he was grateful for the existence and testimony of Orthodox monasticism. The greatest success for Bulgaria was being officially exonerated by the Pope for the so-called "Bulgarian trail," according to which the Bulgarian government was behind the assassination attempt of 13 May 1981.

"Under no circumstances," John Paul II said in Sofia, "did I ever stop loving the Bulgarian people."

The trip to Toronto, Mexico and Guatemala was the first to be planned officially taking the Pope's physical limitations into account. In fact for the first time, the visit began with a rest period of two and a half days on Strawberry Island. Deep in the countryside, John Paul II recovered from the journey and the time difference, and was then ready to meet the numerous young people who had come to meet him, despite the fact that the fears caused by September 11th had not been entirely put to rest.

Several obstacles threatened the celebration of World Youth Day: on the one hand, the Pope's growing frailness; on the other, the climate of fear that came about after September 11th; but in the end, the stubbornness of the "old Pope" who "still felt young," and the courage of the youngsters who had come from 170 countries, made the event possible. The Pope, infected by the cheerful spirit around him, seemed on good form, and more than once he made a joke. "Eighty-two years," he said, to the delight of his audience, "are not the same as 22 or 23 years of age."

He chose the meeting in Toronto to publicly express his "deep shame and sadness" for the harm done by pedophile priests, especially in the United States. Here, Wojtyla gave a message full of optimism. "I am old and a little tired, and you are young, but I identify with your joys and hopes…. I have lived through many dark times, but I am still firmly convinced that no fear or difficulty is big enough to stifle hope."

At the end of the ceremony, John Paul II announced that the next World Youth Day would take place in Cologne, Germany, in 2005. Contrary to what he had said on previous such occasions, the Pope did not say, "I will see you in Cologne." He ended by saying "Jesus is waiting for you in Cologne."

After Canada, he was resolute and determined in his decision to make a stop in Guatemala and Mexico, although his collaborators and doctors had tried to dissuade him from continuing his journey.

He did not want to give up the canonization of the missionary from the Canary Islands, Pedro de Betancur, the humble monk who founded the first literacy school in Latin America, and Juan Diego, the first indigenous saint venerated by the Mexican people, before whom the Virgin of Guadalupe had appeared.

Unlike what had happened during his first visit to Guatemala in 1983 (that time, the President Rios Montt had had 6 death sentences carried out, despite the appeals of John Paul II, who was to

arrive in three days time), this time the President Alfonso Portillo decided to suspend 36 executions, in honor of the Pope.

After just 25 hours in Guatemala, the Pope went to Mexico. Millions of people took to the streets, following the Pope along the route that leads to the Basilica of the Virgin of Guadalupe. There, accompanied by the sound of sea shells and maracas, the Pope made the humble indigenous man Juan Diego into a saint. The ritual dance of 14 Aztec dancers, adorned with beautiful multicolored feathers, marked the main moments of the celebration, during which the Pope requested that "the legitimate aspirations of the indigenous people" be listened to.

John Paul II could not fully enjoy the vast indigenous partly due to his visible tiredness; however, he paid homage to the Virgin of Guadalupe, in whose hands he had placed his Pontificate in January 1979. To the Mexicans, who were glued to their radios, televisions, to the giant screens set up in the streets of the capital, he said, "Mexico needs its indigenous people and the indigenous people need Mexico." The Pope who appeared in Lourdes seemed even more tired: with his face contorted by pain and suffering, Wojtyla knelt before the statue of Our Lady for a long minute; the following day, while he was praying for the sick, the suffering, the pilgrims of Lourdes, he had to interrupt the Mass, gasping "Help me!"

BALTIMORE, October 1995

The Pope walks down the steps of the plane that
has brought him to Maryland from New York.
(pages 90-91)

PORT AU PRINCE, March 1983

Having just arrived at the airport of Haiti,
John Paul II kneels to kiss the ground,
as he always did.

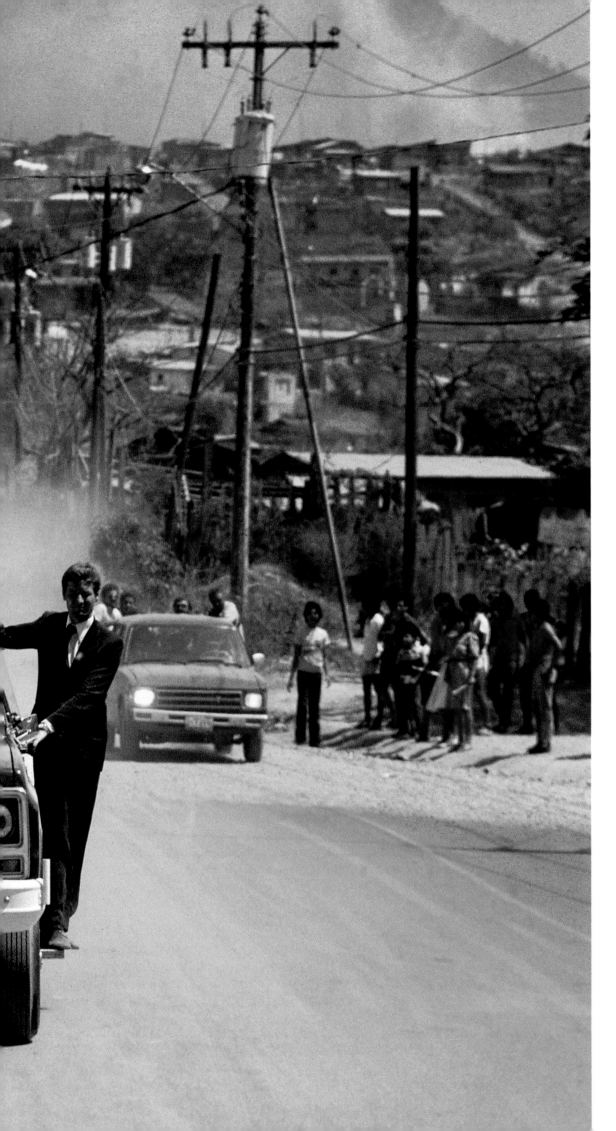

After a ceremony in Honduras, the Papal
motorcade takes a wrong turning and finds
itself in the dusty streets of a small village.

BOMBAY, January 1986

The believers listen to the Pope's speech regarding respect for
different cultures and faiths, essential for the peaceful growth
of all countries.

KATOWICE, June 1983

Torrential rain does not prevent the vast crowd
of fellow Poles to listen to the homily in which
the Pope defends union rights.

GDANSK, June 1987

The Pope returns to Poland in 1987 and,
during the crowded Mass in Gdansk,
he praises Solidarnosc.

(pages 98-99)

MANAGUA, March 1983

During the ceremony he officiated in Nicaragua in
front of a portrait of the leader Sandino, for the
first time the Pope was interrupted during a Mass.

VILNIUS, September 1993

A Lithuanian woman who has rushed to hear
Mass celebrated by the Pope, expresses
her devotion by raising her arms to the sky.

(pages 100-101)

EL SALVADOR, March 1983

For the duration of his trip to San Salvador, armed soldiers escort the Pope and his entourage at all times.

RIO DE JANEIRO, June 1980

It is evening when the Pope returns to Nunziatura, after his meeting with two million people, which the newspapers say is "the largest crowd in the history of Brazil."

CAIRO, February 2000

Observed by President Hosni Mubarak,
two children present the fatigued Pope
with earth in a silver tray.

CAIRO, February 2000

Loud applause greets the arrival of the Pontiff
on a courtesy visit to Mohamed Sayed Tantawi,
the Grand Sheikh of the University of Al-Azhar.

ST. CATHERINE'S MONASTERY, February 2000

During his jubilee pilgrimage to Egypt, the Pope went to the Mount Sinai, where Moses received the Tablets of the Testimony. Visiting St. Catherine's Monastery, where Moses himself saw the "burning bush," the Pope recites a homily in the Olive Garden.

MOUNT NEBO, March 2000

The Pope in contemplation on the slopes of Mount Nebo: this is where Jean Paul II began his Jubilee pilgrimage to the Holy Land.

BETHLEHEM, March 2000

A few feet away from the Basilica of the Nativity,
in Bethlehem's Manger Square, Mass is celebrated
in the presence of the local authorities.

RAMALLAH, March 2000

During the welcome ceremony in the Palestinian
territories, John Paul II thanked President Arafat,
wishing him peace for his people.

DAMASCUS, May 2001

A child gets past security and manages to enter
the courtyard of the Great Omayyad Mosque,
where the Pope is addressing the Muslim
Community.

LVIV, June 2001

The Pope celebrates the divine liturgy
in the Byzantine rite, with beatifications,
at the hippodrome on Stryiska Road,
in Lviv (Lwov), Ukraine.

115

ETCHMIADZIN, September 2001

The meeting between the Patriarch Karekin
and John Paul II during his visit to
Armenia: this was the first time that a
Pontiff had stayed in the residence of the
head of another Church.

POLAND, August 2002

The Pope, returning to his homeland in 2002, is
suffering; but, as always, the children and young
people present provide relief from his pain.

Polish nuns take part in the Mass in Kraków,
the largest ever celebrated in Europe.
Three million people came to see the Pope
in the course of what was to be his last visit
to the land of his birth.

LOURDES, August 2004

With some difficulty, the Pope recited a long
and moving prayer in front of the Cave
of Apparitions at Massabielle.

SOVEREIGN OF A SMALL REALM

In Roman times, the districts to the west of the Tiber developed much more slowly than those on the opposite bank, where the original nucleus of the city was. The trans Tiberim only developed in the imperial era, and the Aurelian walls excluded the Vatican. However, it was precisely there that Christian Rome, almost as though it wished to oppose pagan Rome, had its cultural and ideological center, right from the beginning; it was to become increasingly important, until it came to be the place which represented the physical presence of the head of the Church.

The main body of this government, which acts as a sort of presidency of the council, is the Secretariat of State; its task is to coordinate relations between the various bodies of the Curia itself, as well as those between the Pope and the bishops, the nuncios, governments and ambassadors. The Secretariat of State consists of two sections: the section of general affairs deals with current affairs, relations with the Curia, drawing up documents and supervising the media of the Holy See. The section for relations with States has the task of maintaining diplomatic relations with various governments and international organizations. The Holy See has diplomatic relations with 177 countries.

The Vatican's organizational chart also includes the various congregations that could be compared to ministries. There are nine in all: the congregation for the doctrine of the faith, for the Oriental Churches, for the divine worship and the discipline of the sacraments, the causes of saints, for bishops, the evangelization of peoples, the clergy, for consecrated life and for Catholic education.

From time to time the heads of the various dicasteries or congregations meet before the Pope. These assemblies are the equivalent of a council of ministers, and are presided over by the Cardinal Secretary of State.

Taking into John Paul's considerable activity, an important role during his papacy was played by the Prefecture of the Pontifical House, which prepared all the papal ceremonies in Italy and organized public and private audiences. This was a considerable task: during his pontificate, John Paul II met over three hundred million people!

As for its economic activity, the Vatican State has the Prefecture for Economic Affairs of the Holy See, a kind of finance ministry, and the Administration of the Patrimony of the Apostolic See, which deals with the administration of assets. After

The love of freedom that always distinguished John Paul II immediately became clear, from the first days of his pontificate. As soon as he was elected Pope, he left the Vatican by car, almost in secret, to go and visit his old friend, the Polish Cardinal Deskur, who was in the Gemelli Hospital. Suffice to say that in 24 years, John Paul II spent the equivalent of one tenth of the length of his pontificate outside the Vatican.

Even today, the figure of the Pope is that of monarch, whose absolute power is recognized inside and outside the Vatican. The treaty signed with the Italian state in 1929 confirms that the Pontiff has full temporal sovereignty in the State of the Vatican City. The fundamental law of this State, which was promulgated in February 2001, states that the Pope, as sovereign, has full executive, legislative and judicial powers.

So a Pontiff has three roles: Head of State, and he is received as such in the countries that he visits; Bishop of Rome, and Head of the Universal Church. In order to carry out this triple role, the Pope has his own government, which is the Curia.

full temporal sovereignty...

the financial scandal of the Banco Ambrosiano, which involved the Banca Vaticana, John Paul II asked for total transparency and created a commission of Cardinals which since then, twice a year, meets to present the budget and final balance sheet. One of the most ancient offices of the Curia is the Apostolic Chamber which, led by the Chamberlain, must carry out delicate tasks during the conclave, the period between the death of the Pope and the election of his successor.

In 1996 the Pope published the apostolic constitution *Universi Dominici Gregis* on the vacant seat of the Apostolic See and the election of the Roman pontiff in which he established, in effect, the rules for the election of his successor.

The constitution states that the new Pope must be elected by a maximum of 120 Cardinals who are less than 80 years old; one of the most important innovations of the constitution is in relation to the method of election, which can no longer be by "acclamation." John Paul II's successors will be elected by means of a secret ballot and will become pontiffs only after having obtained a majority vote of two thirds of the Cardinals present.

Another fundamental change was in relation to the accommodation arrangements for the electing Cardinals who, during the election, will no longer inhabit the cramped cells nearby the Sistine Chapel; the Santa Marta residence has been built for them behind the Audience hall; the Cardinals will be taken by bus to the Sistine Chapel and will not be allowed to have contact with anybody else.

Thus the location of the election remains the Sistine Chapel, with its stove, in which the ballots are burned after a round of voting. If a new pope has been elected, the smoke is white; if not, it is black.

The Pope is also the head of the smallest state in the world, which only covers 18 sq, miles (44 sq. km), in which around 2300

people live and work. The millions of visitors that flock to the Vatican each year, out of faith or a love of art, do not have access to the City itself, which lies beyond St. Peter's Basilica. This is a miniature city lacking in nothing: it has a heliport, from which John Paul II left or arrived when coming and going from Castelgandolfo; a train station, where goods trains arrive; a supermarket, which is very sought-after by the Romans as it has excellent VAT-free products; gas stations (gasoline is cheaper in them than in Italy); a pharmacy, which sells prescription medicines that are not found in Italy; a fire station; the headquarters of Radio Vaticana; the *Osservatore Romano*'s printing works, the Vatican Television Center's offices and studios, and finally, an "industrial zone" where there are carpenters, blacksmiths, electricians....

One of the most picturesque spots in this mini-city is the barracks of the Swiss Guard, the so-called "Pope's army," which even has its own beer cellar. The Swiss Guards, whose mission it is to protect the Vatican City, are arranged around the various entrances to the city, wearing a colored uniform traditionally thought to have been designed by Michelangelo.

And then there are the Vatican Museums, which hold matchless artistic treasures, so much so that in 1984 they, together with the Vatican City itself, were put on UNESCO's World Artistic Heritage list. In order to manage with the huge rise in visitors, at the end of the 1990s four floors and new exhibition areas were built.

The Vatican Museums complex is unique in the world thanks to the richness of its artistic treasures, especially religious art; it occupies 428,000 sq. ft (40,000 sq. m) divided among no fewer than 12 museums: to visit them all one, in addition to the queue outside would have to add almost 5 miles (7 km) walking around inside! There is something for everyone here: pieces made by the Etruscans, the Romans, the Greeks, works from the first era of

... the official organ of the Holy See,

Christianity, Pagan Rome, collections of religious art and precious contemporary works of art; the magnificent Rooms and Loggias of Raphael, and the Vatican Library deserve a special mention. In one sense, the Vatican Museums are the result of the relationship that the Popes, over the centuries, have had with art. Indeed, most of the Museums are named after the Pope who decided to collect the works of art and sculptures that they house.

While on the subject, it is interesting to note that in Rome in the early 17th century, there was a renewal in interest in ancient art; consequently, this brought with it a considerable number of artworks as well as a thorough reorganization of the various museums.

In recent decades, thanks to Pope John XXIII the Gregorian Profane and Pius Christian museums were opened. For his part, Paul VI created the historical museum to exhibit precious objects from the ancient Pontifical State; today, this museum holds a collection of modern religious art which includes 740 works by some of the most important artists of our time, including choice works by Matisse, Chagall, Moore and Carrà which depict themes relating to the teachings of the church. Those who enjoy visiting great world museums will enjoy the Pinacoteca (picture gallery), which was opened by Pope Pius XI in 1932. Here visitors can admire works by artists such as Caravaggio, Leonardo, Pinturicchio, Raphael, Rubens, Van Dyck and Titian.

Undoubtedly, however, visitors' main destination is the Sistine Chapel, in which the ceiling and the Last Judgment frescoes by Michelangelo have been stirring unparalleled emotions for centuries. It was here that Cardinal Karol Wojtyla said, after the vote that turned him into the new Pope, "In spite of great difficulties, I accept." It was here that the Pope, during a solemn Mass at the end of the restoration of the Last Judgment, defined the Sistine Chapel "Sanctuary of the Theology of the Body." It was here that

each year, at the beginning of January, the Pope used to baptize about twenty children of different nationalities.

Between 1984 and 1994, the 800,00 sq. ft (750 sq. m) of the ceiling and the 1925 sq ft (180 sq. m) of the Last Judgment were restored. The restoration work, which was financed by Nippon Television Network in Tokyo, surprised the world; this is because contrary to what had been thought, Michelangelo's colors were not dark and dull, but light and bright. People were most struck by the vivid, bright blue, which had been darkened by candle smoke and other atmospheric agents. Practically unknown of by the public, but of great value, is the restoration workshop for the splendid wall hangings that are part of the Vatican's artistic patrimony. In this workshop time seems to stand still: six women, three nuns and three laypeople, spend their life bent over tapestries by the most famous Medieval and Renaissance artists, including Raphael.

But the place which best calls to mind the image of the Pope is St. Peter's Square.

which is published each day in Italian…

It must have been an incredible feeling for the newly elected Pope to see for the first time sunrays lighting up the cobbles of the Roman pavement, made up of the famous "sanpietrini" stones. This square was where St. Peter was martyred. The same square has been on the verge of witnessing the martyrdom of John Paul II.

In effect, the history of the place where the heart of Christianity beats for the whole world, began with a martyrdom: that of the apostle Peter who, it is said, was crucified here upside down, as a sign of humility toward Jesus Christ, between 64 and 67 A. D.; it is also said that he is buried here, about 20 ft (6 m) beneath the spot where the basilica's main altar now stands, surmounted by Bernini's splendid bronze baldachin.

Almost three centuries after the crucifixion, Emperor Constantine had an enormous basilica built at the site of the martyrdom, not only to pay homage to Peter's memory, but also to allow those who wanted to be buried nearby.

When the Papacy returned from Avignon, the Constantine basilica, gleaming with precious works of art and goldsmithery, was by now over a thousand years old, and was close to collapse. Renovations and rough modifications proved to be insufficient. Pope Julius II therefore decided to commission Bramante to design a new church. The demolition and reconstruction work began in 1506 and continued for a century and a half. The radical renewal of the basilica was the result of various designs carried out by the most important artists of the time; it ended, in the mid-17th century, with the basilica that we know today, and with the square that has offered a unique spectacle ever since then. The geometrical perfection is stunning: 284 travertine columns, 53 ft tall, and arranged into 4 rows, 88 pillars and 140 statues of saints, placed on the balustrade, which represent the visual elements of St. Peter's embrace of the world.

The star of the square is the basilica, the façade of which is as large as a football pitch. The cupola by Michelangelo, which tops the basilica, is 140 ft (42.5 m) in diameter; below is the baldachin by Bernini (95ft/29 m), the main altar, and beneath it the tomb of St. Peter.

The square, which is considered Bernini's most successful creation, is dominated by the Egyptian obelisk, which dates from nearly 2000 years ago; it is traditionally believed to be the only witness to Peter's martyrdom, as he was crucified near it. The square is also the best place for observing the most famous windows in the world: those opening on to the central loggia of the basilica, where John Paul II appeared as soon as he was elected, and from where he delivered the *Urbi et Orbi* blessing at Christmas and Easter; and those of his private study, where he appeared every Sunday to recite the Angelus or Regina Coeli.

St. Peter's Square is one of the most admired stages of the world, and one of the most "media friendly."

The eyes of the whole world stare at the roof of the Sistine Chapel when the white smoke indicates that the new Pope has been elected. It was in this square that, once the election had taken place, Karol Wojtyla won over the Italians, by telling them, "I don't know if I can make myself understood in your – in our – Italian language. If I make a mistake, you will correct me." It was in this square, thronged with pilgrims who had come for a general audience, that the Pope was injured by the shots of the terrorist Ali Agca.

The French Cardinal Decourtray has spoken of how, before the Pope visited Lyons, he had warned him that according to an interpretation of the prophesies of Nostradamus, he could be the victim of an assassination attempt. The Pope had replied, "I assure you, Your Eminence, that nowhere is more dangerous that St. Peter's Square."

THE SALA REGIA ("ROYAL HALL")

One of the most highly-awaited events at the beginning of each new year was the Pope's meeting with the diplomatic corps in the sumptuous setting of the Sala Regia, the vast hall decorated with frescoes by Vasari, situated at the entrance to the Sistine Chapel.

THE SALA CLEMENTINA ("CLEMENTINE HALL")

At Christmas, an exchange of greetings always took place with the Cardinals present at the Vatican.

(pages 132-133)

THE SISTINE CHAPEL

The Pope leads the inauguration ceremony of the
Sistine Chapel, which has been restored to its original
splendor after a lengthy process.

THE CENTRAL BALCONY

On 1st January 2000, with St. Peter's Square
packed with the faithful, including many children,
the Pope conducts the Jubilee of Young People.

BERNINI'S ALTAR

A solemn ceremony beneath the baldachin
by Bernini closes the business of the Cardinals'
Consistory.

THE STATUE

The enormous statue of St. Peter towers over
thousands of clerics who have gathered in the
square to celebrate the Jubilee.

(pages 140-141)

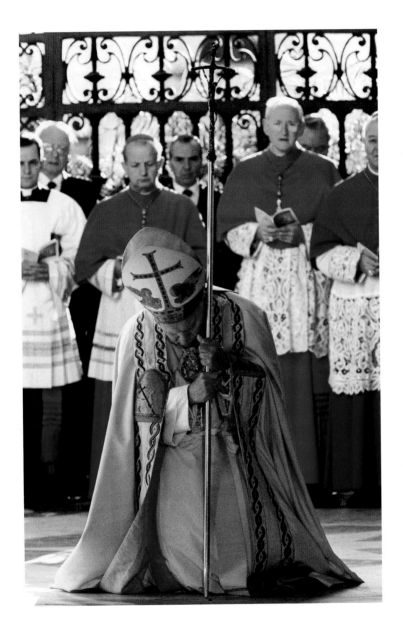

THE HOLY DOOR

The Pope, in pain and emotionally moved, yet sustained by his
faith and mysticism, having knocked on the Holy Door of St.
Peter's Basilica, stays kneeling for around two minutes. It is
11.25 p.m. on 24 December 1999.

IN·HONOREM·PRINCIPIS·APOST·PAVLVS·V·BVRGHESIVS·ROMANVS·PONT·MAX·AN·M D

JUBILEE 2000

A view of St. Peter's
Square on Christmas
night. The Mass in the
Basilica, celebrated by
the Pope, officially
opens the Jubilee
Year of 2000.

THE BASILICA

In January 2001 the Pope
bows before the Holy Door
of St. Peter's Basilica; with
the closing of this door,
after 379 days of
celebrations, the Great
Jubilee ends.

(pages 146-147)

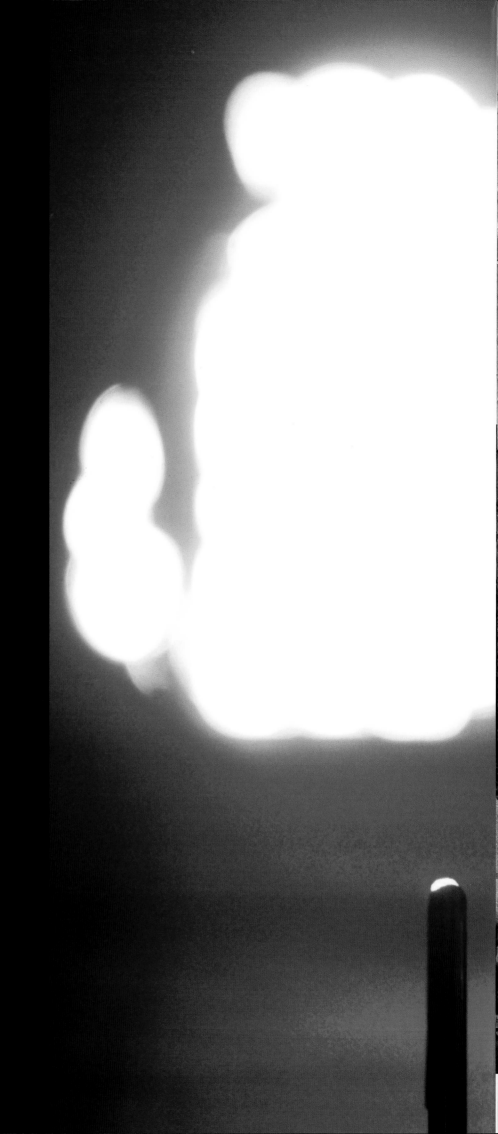

THE DAYS
OF PAIN

In recent years the global stage that for over fifteen years had been the backdrop to the hurricane Wojtyla – "the athlete of God, the marathon-runner of God" – had become the backdrop to an icon of suffering.

The first time that we saw John Paul II leaning on a walking stick, after an operation on his femur in 1994, was a shock. Perhaps it was for him too, as he had scaled so many mountains and with his swift, big strides had broken down walls and crossed thresholds that had never been crossed before. Over time the Pope managed to accept his intolerable dependence on that walking stick, by using it ironically: he began to play with it, swinging it in front of the young people of Manila, to the sound of music, or shaking it threateningly to "cruel, always indiscreet" journalists. Despite the increasingly visible tremor in his hands – due to Parkinson's disease, which had been rumored for years without actually being confirmed – and despite his increasingly unsteady step, the Pope had continued to walk the streets of the world. His staff had gradually become his support. More and more infirm, he clutched onto it with all his strength.

The merciless progression of the illness bent his back, took away his gestures, which had conquered audiences all over the world, but never took away the light in his gaze, which was always penetrating. Above all, it never managed to take away his true strength: interior strength. Unyielding, he continued his mission. At moments when he appeared as a tireless pilgrim, forms of "assistance" also appeared that caused a sensation each time. How can we forget the time when, upon arriving at Baku, Azerbaijan in May 2002, he did not get off the plane using his legs: for the first time he was helped down by a lift and, also for the first time on an airport runway, the mobile platform appeared. He had begun using it in the Vatican two years previously, especially for crossing the central nave of St. Peter's Basilica. At the end of that journey, which finished in Bulgaria, Metropolitan Simeon of the Bulgarian oerthodox Church, said "To us he seemed like the suffering Christ, tell him to stop . . ."

John Paul II, who was by now aware of his suffering, did not stop; however, the uncertainty surrounding his future began to affect his plans. Three months later, his difficult trip to Toronto, Guatemala and Mexico was almost interrupted. Having taken part in World Youth Day in Toronto he arrived in Guatemala, completely shattered. Right up to the last moment, in Mexico, it was feared that he would have to quickly return to the Vatican. Despite the fact that he

was increasingly a prisoner in his own body, the Pope continued his journeys. In September 2003 the "mobile throne," which had already been used in the Vatican, made an appearance in Bratislava. Much more worrying was the Pope's inability to read out his own messages. He had already been helped with delivering his speeches in Armenia in September 2001, and the year after in Azerbaijan and Bulgaria; but in Slovakia, his difficulties with diction gave us a first glimpse at the sight of a mute Pope. This scene was seen by the world during the celebrations for the 25th anniversary of his election, when on the first of many occasions Monsignor Leonardo Sandri, a substitute from the Secretariat of State, acted as the voice of the Pope. Yet the great communicator, even in silence, continued to instil strength in the faithful; for them, his physical limitations, which were totally incorporated with his ministry, had increased his greatness. A perfect example was the reaction of the sick at Lourdes, to where the Pope, "a sick person among the sick" managed to bring consolation and even hope. During that last journey of his, John Paul II, in great difficulty, asked for help in Polish during the celebration of the Mass. Exhausted from reading his message to the sick, which he wanted to read out in its entirety, he murmured *"Musza siconczyc"*: "I must reach the end."

The previous day, at the Our Lady of Lourdes Grotto, he had wanted to kneel, but his legs would not support him: live in front

the suffering Christ, tell him to stop. . . . "

of the television cameras, we saw him slip from the kneeler, about to fall, until he was helped up. Sitting down again, the Pope seemed exhausted: bent over from tiredness, he put his head between his hands. The television cameras captured the tears on his face. Perhaps partly due to his extreme emotion, the Pope could not manage to read a few lines dedicated to the sick. Cardinal Roger Etchegaray did so in his place.

It was at Lourdes, in the midst of the palpably deep emotion, that John Paul II said, "Dear brothers and sisters who are sick, with you I share a time of life marked by physical suffering ... here I feel, with emotion, that I have reached the end of my pilgrimage." This was an ambiguous phrase, which once again fired up the debate regarding the Pope's possible resignation, which had already accompanied his calvary.

He himself, however, never left us in any doubt as to his intentions. "Did Christ get down from the cross?" he once said to a cardinal, and "The strength to continue is not my problem, but the problem of those who, by mysterious design, called me to be the servant of the servants of God." In his last years, whether in the Vatican or traveling out in the world, John Paul II appeared as a man who suffers like one of us, rather than as a champion exhausted at the finishing line. This suffering humanity of the Pope's meant that on the night of 1 February 2005, after the announcement that he had been urgently admitted to the Gemelli Hospital, the world waited with bated breath. The first Vatican statement issued spoke of acute laryngotracheitis: it was clear to everyone that the Pope was near to death through suffocation.

In his last book, *Memory and Identity,* published just as he entered the Gemelli Hospital, the Pope describes how, when he was first admitted to the Roman clinic, on 13 May 1981 after the assassination attempt, "I was practically already on the other side." Hanging between life and death for several hours, the man who was then "the globetrotter of faith" could not have imagined that he would return to Gemelli Hospital eight times; the last of these was on 24 February 2005, when he suffered new respiratory attacks that forced doctors to perform a tracheotomy at 8.30 p.m. that same day.

The first hospital stay in February had lasted ten days, during which the Pope had recovered from the laryngotracheitis. On Sunday 6 February, John Paul II wanted to appear behind the windows of the room on the tenth floor of the hospital to recite the Angelus. The message was read out by Monsignor Leonardo Sandri, who also recited the prayer. In the end, the Pope delivered the blessing but his voice was shaky and metallic, as though it was in fact a recording from a previous occasion; the Vatican later denied this.

The Pope himself affectionately defined the Gemelli Hospital as "Vatican No. 3" since, after the Vatican and Castelgandolfo, this was the place in which he had spent the greatest number of days. His emergency admission on 1 February at about 11 p.m. was the beginning of the final phase of his pontificate. From that evening onward, with a brief interruption of 14 days during which the Pope had returned to the Vatican, the eyes of the world were fixed on the tenth floor rooms, which had always been kept ready for the Pope since 1981, until the night of Sunday, April 3rd, 2005.

Television cameras from the major international networks were focuses 24 hours a day toward those windows, together with the photographers' lenses. In all the messages written during his two stays in hospital, John Paul II thanked the faithful all over the world who had filled the churches to pray for his health.

Perhaps conscious of all the speculation surrounding his true capacity to lead the Church, he repeated that, even from the Gemelli, he would carry out his mission as universal pastor, asking for the help of everyone so that he could carry on for as long as God wished. When he woke up from the anaesthetic after his tracheotomy operation, he asked for pen and paper and wrote "But I am still *Totus Tuus,*" entrusting himself once again to the Virgin Mary.

They also say that, with his well-known sense of humor, when the doctors told him before the operation that it would only be a small procedure, he replied, "Small for who?", and that after coming out of the operating room and seeing the cannula, he wrote, "But what have you done to me?"

ROME, March 2002

Fatigued by the Easter celebrations and affected by his illness, during an intense Via Crucis, the exhausted Pope holds the cross with one hand and leans on the railings with the other.

(pages 152-153)

BAKU, May 2002

Arriving in Azerbaijan, after the welcome ceremony at the airport, the Pope's hands seek some support to alleviate the strain of having to stand.

(pages 154-155)

SOFIA, May 2002

After meeting President Parvanov, the Pontiff is supported by his two special secretaries, Msgr. Stanislaw Dziwisz and Msgr. Mieczyslaw Mokrzycki.

March 6th 2005

After only two weeks, having suffered a relapse. John Paul II is once again taken to the Gemelli Hospital, where he then underwent a tracheotomy.

March 12th 2005

On his second return from hospital
to the Vatican, the Pope traveld in a van:
it skims around the colonnade, crosses
the deserted square and passes
the windows of the Papal Apartments,
which are still dark.

March 27th 2005

Tears and distress among the 75,000-strong
crowd of the faithful gathered in St. Peter's
Square to receive the *Urbi et Orbi* blessing.
For the first time from the beginning
of his pontificate, the Pope is unable to deliver
his Easter message.

"Why have you abandoned me?"
Nobody will ever know what thoughts
troubled John Paul II in those moments.
The Pope, by nature a vigorous, active
man, shows a gesture of frustration when
faced with the fact that he cannot speak.
This would be the Pontiff's last public
appearance.

The Vatican City, April 3rd, 4th, 5th, 2005.

Peace has come over the face of the man, Karol Josef Wojtyla, whose agony was long and painful, but full of that courage that the Pope brought to the world in a unique example of humanity. Pope John Paul II passed away in the evening of April 2nd, at 9.37 p.m. in his private apartments; the following day, he was taken to the Sala Clementina in the Apostolic Palace (left), where members of the Roman Curia, the authorities and the consular corps paid their respects. The pontiff, with a white miter on his head and dressed in the red papal tiara, has a relaxed, serene expression, finally abandoned by the pain, by the suffering that millions of people around the world have followed and shared, minute by minute. At 5.30pm on April 4th, the body is taken to St. Peter's. The opening of the doors to the Basilica, which was planned for 9 p.m. is brought forward by over an hour, given the vast crowds of faithful who are waiting. The procession continues for almost the whole night – it is thought that every hour, 15,000 people paid their respects to the Pontiff – and begins again at 5 a.m.

2nd - 7th April 2005

Tens of thousands of faithful of every background and origin do not abandon the Pope at his most difficult moments, and nor do they after the end: they continue to pray day and night. All are in deep in contemplation. Many offer spontaneous demonstrations of their respect, holding on to each other as if to stop themselves from feeling abandoned. Each is deeply absorbed, but all are part of one single spirit that murmurs the world's immense love for the John Paul II the Great – a title of recognition the world has already accorded Pope Jon Paul II.

April 8th 2005

Heads of state, kings and queens,
presidents of international organizations
observe the passing of the coffin. Some
200 "powerful of the earth" are there to
represent their own nations and
institutions in an expression of grief that
unites the entire planet.

This is the day of the solemn funeral rites. During the Mass officiated by Cardinal Ratzinger, shouts of "Santo Subito", meaning "Saint now," go up from the roaring crowd. It is thought that 3 million people watched the ceremony in Rome alone, 300,000 of whom were in St. Peter's Square. The Pope is buried in the crypt, in an unadorned coffin. Polish flags flutter in the strong wind that blew that morning: many hundreds of the Pope's compatriots – many of them coming from other countries, such as the United States – came to attend the ceremony.

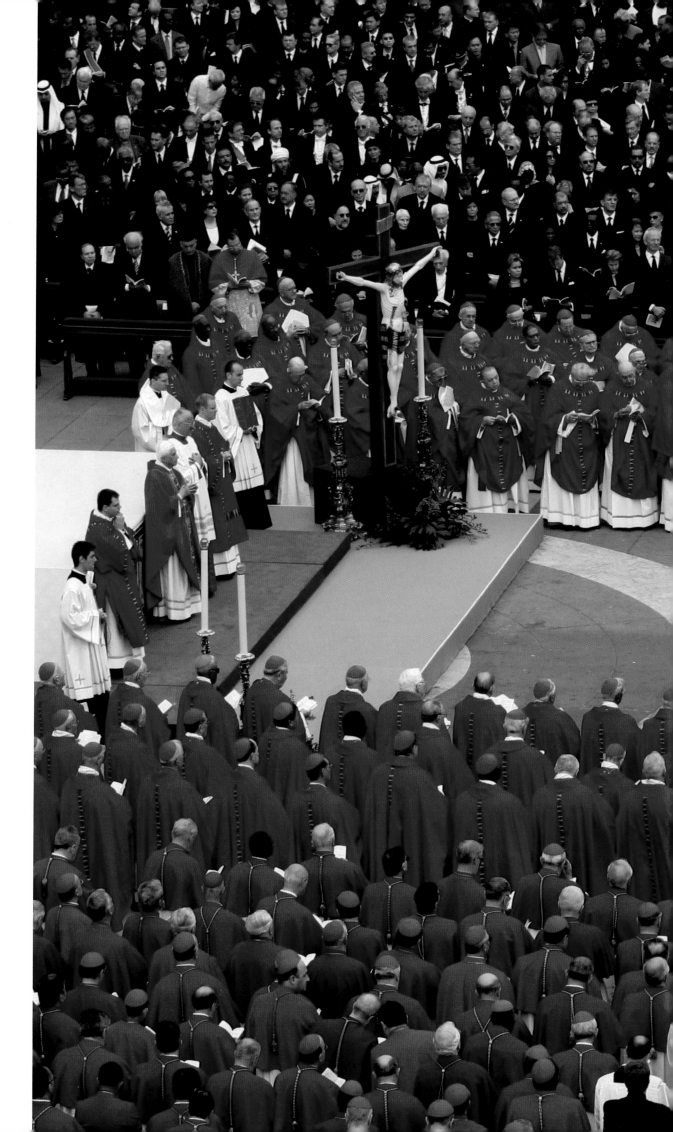

8th April 2005

Patriarchs from the Eastern Rite Churches pay their respects with incense over the simple cypress coffin, laid on a carpet, before the ordered rows of the ecclesiastical and civil dignitaries from all over the world. Everyone followed the funeral mass with great concentration, but the homily was to be interrupted by no less than 13 rounds of applause, echoing around the square.

Acknowledgments

Biagio Agnes, Valentina Alazraki, Andrea Andermann, Riccardo Auci, Roberto Bettoni, Egildo Biocca,
Raul Bonarelli, Don Giorgio Bruni, Camillo Cibin, Clara Colelli, Giuseppe D' Amico,
Alessandro Di Napoli, Mons. Stanislao Dziwisz, Franco Fegatelli, Mons. John Patrick Foley,
Alberto Gasparri, Suor Giovanna Gentili, Dott. Domenico Giani, Giancarlo Giuliani, Angelo Gugel,
Hubert Henrotte, Padre Federico Lombardi, Arturo Mari, Chiara Mariani, Mons. Piero Marini, Alain Mingam,
Joaquin Navarro-Valls, Michele Neri, Franco Origlia, Mons. Pierfranco Pastore, Laura Riccioni,
Padre Leonardo Sapienza, Angelo Scelzo, Francesco Sforza, Vittorio Storaro, Roberto Tucci,
Vik Van Brantegem, Marjorie Weeke

A special thanks to Ada Masella.

VMB Publishers®
An imprint of White Star, Italy

© 2005 White Star S.p.a.
Via Candido Sassone, 22/24 -
13100 Vercelli, Italy
www.whitestar.it

Photographs © Gianni Giansanti

Translation: Studio Vecchia, Milano

ISBN 88-540-0360-3

REPRINTS:
1 2 3 4 5 6   09 08 07 06 05

Printed in Spain